Reading American History

The Boston Tea Party

Written by Melinda Lilly
Illustrated by Patrick O'Brien

Educational Consultants

Kimberly Weiner, Ed.D
Betty Carter, Ed.D

Rourke
Publishing LLC
Vero Beach, Florida 32963

www.rourkepublishing.com

Designer: Elizabeth J. Bender

Library of Congress Cataloging-in-Publication Data

Lilly, Melinda.
   The Boston Tea Party / Melinda Lilly; illustrated by Patrick O'Brien.
      p. cm. — (Reading American history)
   Summary: A simple description of the 1773 event known as the Boston Tea Party, at
which American colonists dumped English tea into the sea rather than pay taxes on it.
   ISBN 1-58952-357-1
   1. Boston Tea Party, 1773—Juvenile literature. [1. Boston Tea Party, 1773.] I. O'Brien,
illus. II. Title.

E215.7 .L55 2002
973.3'115—dc21   2002017843

Cover Illustration: One of the Sons of Liberty throws a tea chest
overboard during the Boston Tea Party.

Printed in the USA

Time Line

Help students follow this story by introducing important events in the Time Line.

1767   Tea is taxed in the colonies as part of the Townshend Acts.

1770   Five Americans die as a result of the Boston Massacre.

1773   The Tea Act lowers the tax on English tea.

1773   The Boston Tea Party

1775   The Battle of Concord and Lexington

1776   The Declaration of Independence

In 1773, **England** rules **America**.
Three ships dock at **Boston**.

Ships from England come to Boston.

Many tea chests sit on the ships.

Tea chests

England says America must pay **tax** on the tea.

No! says **Samuel Adams**.

Samuel Adams in Boston

Yes! says the **governor**.

England wants him to get the tea off the ships.

The governor in Boston

Samuel Adams has a plan.

Adams tells his plan.

Adams and 50 Americans try to dress as **Native Americans**.

The Americans want no one to know who they are.

The men rush onto the ships at night.

Time for the **Boston Tea Party**

The men dump the tea into the sea.

Now the governor cannot sell the tea.

No tea on the ship!

There will be no tax for England,

just tea for the fish!

A fish sips tea.

Word List

Adams, Samuel (AD emz, SAM you el)—Born in 1722, Samuel Adams was a leader of the American Revolution.

America (uh MER ih kuh)—The land that is now the United States

Boston (BAW stun)—The capital of the state of Massachusetts, Boston was an important town in the colonies.

Boston Tea Party (BAW stun TEE PAR tee)—An event in 1773, when Americans dumped tea into Boston harbor instead of paying tax on it

England (ING glund)—Part of the country of Great Britain and the United Kingdom

governor (GUV ur nur)—The head of government for a state or other area

Native Americans (NAY tiv uh MER ih kunz)—Members of the peoples native to North America; American Indians

tax (TAKS)—Money that has to be paid to a government by its citizens

Books to Read

Burgan, Michael. *The Boston Tea Party*. Compass Point Books, 2000.

Edwards, Pamela Duncan. *Boston Tea Party*. Putnam Publishing Group, Juvenile, 2001.

Furstinger, Nancy. *The Boston Tea Party*. Bridgestone Books, 2002.

Kroll, Steven. *The Boston Tea Party*. Holiday House, 2000.

Websites to Visit

www.whitehouse.gov/kids/dreamteam/samueladams.html

http://odur.let.rug.nl/~usa/H/1990/ch2_p8.htm

www.historyplace.com/unitedstates/revolution/index.html

www.pbs.org/ktca/liberty/chronicle/episode1.html

Index